INTRODU

This booklet arose from a series of
1987. They were intended for those who m....
assertion that belief in creation, as described in the Bible, is
'unscientific' but who may not be aware that this claim is
unjustified. Its purpose is to give an outline indicating firstly
what the Bible teaches, secondly that this is fundamentally
different from the theories generally taught in the world today,
thirdly that there are serious objections to these theories and
finally that true science and the Bible are not in conflict.

Without apology, the starting point is faith in the inspired,
infallible Word of God. 'Holy men of God spake as they were
moved by the Holy Ghost' (2 Pet.1.21); and 'all scripture is given
by inspiration of God' (2 Tim.3.16). Although the Bible is not a
secular history book nor a scientific textbook the Christian
believes that what God inspired men to write could not be, and
has not been proven to be, in error. Recent discoveries in
archaeology are now generally recognised by unbelievers to be in
harmony with much of biblical history which a few generations
ago critics regarded as pure myth; in general, however, only
believers acknowledge that recent scientific discoveries are also
in harmony with the Bible.

Proper scientific theories are developed to account for
observed facts and can be tested. Because creation took place
before recorded history the original processes involved cannot be
observed nor can theories about them be tested. Science and
reason are great God-given gifts which enable men to observe the
wonderful workings of the created world and to discover some of
the laws of nature by which God normally orders all things.
Those who believe the Bible are able to propose an account of
the history of the natural world based on two sets of information:
firstly the special acts of God recorded in the Bible, and
secondly the facts obtained from scientific observation of the

present world, which include the known laws of nature. Those who do not believe in these special acts of God can only propose an account based on the observed facts and the belief that everything has come about solely by the operation of the present laws of nature, without the intervention of God. Thus everything is interpreted according to one belief or the other. Inevitably the two accounts are totally irreconcilable. Many have attempted to reconcile them, but underlying all such attempts there is an implicit, if not explicit, denial of some of the important truths and basic doctrines of the Bible.

The theories which neglect God and what He has told us about His great acts, and which do not take account of man's spiritual nature, are inevitably disastrously wrong. The Bible says that all creation shows the power and glory of its Creator (Psa.19.1; Psa.104.24); those who are not thankful, and do not glorify Him will be without excuse in the day of judgment (Rom.1.18-25).

There is much good literature available today for those who wish to pursue the subject more deeply. Some of this literature is listed in Appendix C; the scientific observations herein which support the biblical position are largely attributable to these sources. Because the booklet is about science, as well as the Bible, scientific knowledge will inevitably help in understanding parts of it; some of the more detailed scientific points have been dealt with separately in appendices for this reason.

The author wishes to acknowledge the valuable advice which he has received from Dr.P.M.Rowell.

Creation

THE BIBLE AND SCIENCE

By
JOHN BARKER

GOSPEL STANDARD TRUST PUBLICATIONS

1993

12(b) Roundwood Lane, Harpenden, Herts. AL5 3DD

ENGLAND

ISBN 1 897837 01 1

Printed in Great Britain at Flair Press, Northampton

CONTENTS

CHAPTER 1

WHAT THE BIBLE TEACHES

The Bible states that God maintains and upholds all things by His power (Col.1.16,17; Heb.1.2,3). This ongoing control of the world is by God's laws of nature, many of which have been discovered by true scientific investigation. These laws do not appear to change and are ideally suited to their purpose; this should be expected since God is unchangeable (Mal.3.6; Jas.1.17) and infinitely wise (Psa.147.5; Rom.11.33). These laws do not however account for the coming into being of the world nor for some of the major changes it has undergone; the Bible says that these things are due to acts of God's almighty power on four different occasions. Each of these four events were of tremendous significance, far more than is perhaps generally appreciated even by those who believe the Bible fully.

The first was God's original creation of all things in which sinless man was placed in an earthly paradise. Three times after this God acted to change this creation radically because of man's sin. These changes were when:

– God cursed all creation because of the disobedience of Adam. This event is known as the 'Fall'.

– God brought about world-wide destruction and change by means of water because of the almost universal wickedness of man. This event is known as the 'Flood'.

– God confounded men's language at Babel because of more great sin.

The Bible presents all four events as historical facts. In many parts of the Bible there are references to them directly or by implication and much of what is said would be neither valid nor consistent unless they were indeed facts. Moreover if only some of these events were factual the believer could not account for the world as it is today, it is so different from the world of Genesis 1 & 2.

The following sections examine what the Bible teaches about these four events.

1. *The Original Creation.*

The Bible says that:

– God created all things 'in the beginning'. This is clearly stated in Genesis 1, but it is most important to appreciate that the whole Bible is based on this. This message is not only given directly but is also implied throughout the Bible. It is clear from Jesus' own words and deeds that this was a basic truth to Him; see for example His teaching on divorce in Mark 10.2-9. His apostles' teaching is based on the same truth as for example in 1 Cor.11.9 which refers to the woman being created for the man. Indeed it is also clear that the Lord Jesus Christ, the Son of God was Himself the Creator (John 1.3; Col.1.16; Eph.3.9; Heb.1.2). To deny that God created all natural things at the beginning of time would involve the rejection of the greater part of the Bible, not just the early chapters of Genesis. The list of direct references to divine creation given in the footnote below*, although not exhaustive, is given at length because of the great importance of this foundational truth of the Bible.

---

* Gen.1 (whole chapter); Ex.20.11; Deut.4.32; 1 Sam.2.8; 1 Chr.16.26; Neh.9.6; Job 38.1-11; Psalms 8.3; 19.1-6; 24.1,2; 33.6-9; 89.11,12; 95.3-6; 102.25; 104 (whole Psalm); 148.5,6; Prov.3.19; 8.22-29; Isa.40.28; 44.24; 45.12; 48.13; 66.2; Jer.10.12; 32.17; 51.15; Amos 4.13; 5.8; Jonah 1.9; Zech.12.1; Mal.2.10; Matt.19.4 & 8; Mark 10.6; 13.19; Luke 11.40; John 1.10; 17.24; Acts 4.24; 7.50; 14.15; 17.24; Rom.1.20; 1 Cor.8.6; Heb.11,3; 1 Pet.4.19; 2 Pet.3.5; Rev.4.11; 10.6.

– Everything was created 'by the word of God' (Heb.11.3), 'He spake and it was done' (Psa.33.9). He said 'Let there be light, and there was light' (Gen.1.3) and each further act of creation is recorded in the same way in this first chapter of the Bible.

– Everything that God created was very good. God who is perfect said this (Gen.1.31). It was good naturally, it was designed and worked perfectly from the beginning, unlike things that men design; everything was beautiful and in harmony; it was good morally, there was no sin, no evil, no trouble. It was indeed an earthly paradise.

– Everything was made in six days. Many have tried to reconcile this record with the theory of evolution by suggesting that these days were very long indefinite periods of time. If this were so why would the Bible insist that each day had an evening and a morning (Gen.1.5,8,13,19,23,31)? Why would God, speaking personally from Mount Sinai in the hearing of all Israel, tell them to rest one (natural) day in seven as He had done at the creation (Ex.20.11)? If the sixth and seventh days were long indefinite periods could Adam's age have been given so precisely (Gen.5.3-5)? It should be noted that even if the 'days' of Gen.1 had been long periods of time the theory of evolution could still not be reconciled with the Bible. The theory of evolution supposes a different sequence of origins from that given in Genesis 1 and follows this with progressive improvement from primitive, animal beginnings; the Bible, on the other hand, tells throughout of perfect beginnings followed by degradation, morally and physically.

– God set waters 'above the firmament' (Gen.1.6,7). 'God called the firmament Heaven' (Gen.1.8). Heaven in a physical sense is the expanse above the earth, namely, the sky. The sky extends from the earth's atmosphere to the remotest star. These waters appear to have been of outstanding importance as will be seen in chapter 4.

– God made each living thing 'after his kind' (Gen.1.12,21,24). These 'kinds' are God's families of creatures. There was probably, for example, a dog family; there are many varieties of dogs but they can generally breed together and produce dogs; they cannot breed with other families and produce fertile offspring. Development of varieties clearly does occur within families, demonstrating the richness of the genetic heritage with which God endowed His creatures. There is no satisfactory evidence to show that the boundaries of God's families can be successfully crossed.

– 'God created man in His own image' (Gen.1.27; 5.1; 9.6; 1 Cor.11.7; Jas.3.9). Adam and Eve were originally without sin and were capable, as no other creature, of communion with God (Gen.2.7). Man has a soul which will live for ever, unlike other creatures (Eccl.3.21; Matt.10.28; Heb.9.27); men of all races and tribes have a religious instinct. God gave man dominion over all other creatures (Gen.1.26), He gave him faculties and abilities no other creatures were to have: man alone can properly walk erect on two feet, make and use tools, musical instruments, utensils, clothes, weapons, means of transport, and make fire and cook. Only man of all God's creatures has the gift of being able to use words (God's own means of creation) and language to convey complex ideas. Adam was a fully developed intelligent man, probably superior to modern man whose natural state has been sadly affected in many ways by sin; his immediate descendants are recorded as raising crops, keeping livestock, working in brass and iron (long before the 'iron age'!), and making and playing musical instruments (Gen.4.2,20,21,22); there were giants (Gen.6.4) and lives were very long (Gen.5). If inferior men existed in prehistoric times they were most likely degenerate descendants after Babel.

– Creation was a finished work: 'The heavens and the earth were finished, and all the host of them. And on the seventh day God ended His work which He had made' (Gen.2.1,2). 'The works were finished from the foundation of the world' (Heb.4.3). Creation was completed from the outset; it was not to evolve gradually.

This earthly paradise was short-lived, probably very brief since Adam and Eve had been commanded to multiply (Gen.1.28) but apparently had not yet had children.

2. *The Curse.*

God gave Adam many good things and just one negative command: 'but of the tree of knowledge of good and evil, thou shalt not eat of it: for in the day that thou eatest thou shalt surely die' (Gen.2.17). Under temptation by the serpent Eve broke this commandment and Adam followed her (Gen.3.6). Because of this disobedience God pronounced and put into effect a curse which had dire consequences for all creation:

– The serpent was cursed above every beast of the field and condemned to go on his belly and to eat dust (Gen.3.14).

– The woman was condemned to greatly increased conception, to bringing forth children in sorrow, and to subjection to her husband (Gen.3.16).

– The ground was cursed and was to bring forth thereafter thorns and thistles (Gen.3.17,18 & 5.29).

– The man was condemned to hard work and sorrow (Gen.3.17,19).

God put into effect the penalty 'thou shalt surely die'; what God says He is sure to perform. Spiritual death entered and communion with God was lost, shame and fear entered as well as sorrow (Gen.3.10), man became subject to physical death (Gen.3.19) and he was driven out of the wonderful garden of Eden (Gen.3.24).

It is clear from what has already been said that physical changes took place affecting men, women, animals, plants and the ground, all because of the sin of man. Rom.8.20-22 says that all creation now groans in bondage.

It would only be possible to speculate how the serpent and other animals were physically changed, but we do know that originally all had been given a herbal diet by God (Gen.1.30). They would have been given the appropriate physical characteristics, such as teeth and digestion, to go with this whereas there is no doubt that many of them now have appropriate physical characteristics to kill and eat other animals, and even man; 'enmity' between man and the serpent was part of the curse (Gen.3.15).

The Bible teaches that all men have descended from Adam; all have inherited the death sentence from him and all are born sinners (Gen.3.20; Psa.51.5; Rom.5.12; 1 Cor.15.22). It also teaches that God's people will ultimately be restored in 'new heavens and a new earth' (Isa.65.17-25 & 11.6-9) to 'righteousness unto eternal life by Jesus Christ our Lord' (Rom.5.21). Commentators generally believe that Gen.3.15 is the first prophecy that Jesus would come to earth to suffer so that this might be fulfilled.

The world then became a very different place, no longer a paradise, now that there was death, sorrow, pain, fear and every kind of trouble as a direct consequence of sin. In this changed world life greatly multiplied but so did the wickedness of man.

The original creation as changed by the Fall lasted from Adam to Noah. The Bible systematically records the generations from Adam to Noah and the number of years between each: 'Adam lived an hundred and thirty years, and begat ... Seth: ... Seth lived an hundred and five years, and begat Enos: ...' and so on until Noah (Gen.5). Adding these intervals together gives some 1600 years for this period of the world's history.

3. *The Flood.*

God brought about tremendous destruction and further change by what is called the Flood, or Deluge. The destructive power of water has been seen in many large scale floods in recent times with great loss of life, buildings and vegetation, but this flood was of immeasurably greater consequence in these and other respects than any other flood the world has ever known.

The Bible records that 'the windows of heaven were opened' and it poured with rain for forty days and at the same time 'all the fountains of the great deep were broken up' (Gen.7.11,12). These waters from above and beneath were sufficient to cause a worldwide flood covering all the high hills and even the mountains (Gen.7.19,20 & 8.9). These were no ordinary rains or fountains, only an act of God Himself could do this; He has told us that this is exactly what it was: 'behold, I, even I, do bring a flood of waters upon the earth' (Gen.6.17). God's purpose was clear: 'to destroy all flesh, wherein is the breath of life, from under heaven' (Gen.6.17), and His reason for it was also clear: 'God saw that the wickedness of man was great in the earth, and that every imagination of the thoughts of his heart was only evil continually' (Gen.6.5) and 'The earth also was corrupt before God, and the earth was filled with violence' (Gen.6.11). Men had become so evil that they were not fit to live; only Noah 'found grace in the eyes of the Lord' (Gen.6.8). He alone was a 'just man' and 'walked with God' (Gen.6.9).

Noah and seven of his family were saved in the ark. God had warned him and directed him to build the ark and to take with him into the ark two of every sort of animal and bird 'after their kind', the 'kinds' of creation, male and female; just sufficient to provide for the repopulation of the earth after the Flood (Gen.6.13-21). Clean beasts and birds were to be taken in sevens to allow for sacrifice, and perhaps food, in the initial period immediately after the Flood (Gen.7.2,3 & 8.20). Noah was given the faith and energy to undertake the great enterprise of building this large ship or barge. Other people must have ridiculed him perhaps more than they do today those who believe that the Bible record of these things is literally true; they continued about their normal affairs 'until the flood came, and took them all away' as Jesus confirmed (Matt.24.39 & Luke 17.26,27). By his act of faith, Noah 'condemned the world' (Heb.11.7).

The ark was larger than any ship built before 1858. Building it in those days would have been a very long job; it may have taken the 120 years of Gen.6.3, but however long it took 'the longsuffering of God waited in the days of Noah, while the ark was a preparing' (1 Pet.3.20). This ark was necessary because the Flood was to be a worldwide catastrophe from which there would be no other means of escape. Had the Flood destroyed only part of the world, as many have suggested, life could have survived without the ark. The proportions of the ark were ideal for its task, naval architects today could not do better; this should not surprise us as it was designed by God whose 'understanding is infinite' (Psa.147.5). It had the right proportions to float with comparative stability on turbulent seas, and its size (Gen.6.15) was more than large enough to carry all the known species of animals in the world.

'The waters prevailed upon the earth an hundred and fifty days' (Gen.7.24) and then dried up in about another six months (Gen.8.4,13). It even took about 74 days after the ark came to rest before the level of the waters fell enough for the tops of the mountains to become visible (Gen.8.4,5). This is a further confirmation of the vast extent of this flood.

The waters accomplished the purpose for which God had sent

them, 'all flesh died that moved upon the earth, both of fowl, and
of cattle, and of beast, and of every creeping thing that creepeth
upon the earth, and every man' (Gen.7.21), except the occupants
of the ark (Gen.7.23). The other creatures were again involved in
the suffering for man's sin; billions of creatures, many of them
no doubt fleeing for their lives, were overtaken by the Flood and
drowned or crushed to death by the immense quantities of rock,
soil, and vegetation being swept before the troubled waters which
soon became a shoreless ocean.

The destruction and change which all this brought about was
such that the Bible states that 'the old world', 'the world that then
was...perished' (2 Pet.2.5 & 3.6). The world after the Flood was
a very different place in many respects; much harsher and even
less like the original paradise. Some of these differences and the
question of where the waters came from and where they went to
will be examined in chapter 4.

God promised Noah that He would never destroy the world
again by water (Gen.9.11), and confirmed this promise in
Isa.54.9. He gave the rainbow as a token of this promise
(Gen.9.12-17). He promised that He would 'not again curse the
ground any more for man's sake' and that 'while the earth
remaineth, seedtime and harvest, and cold and heat, and summer
and winter, and day and night shall not cease' (Gen.8.21,22). As
God is faithful to His promises (Deut.7.9; Heb.10.23) there have
been no further acts of God causing destruction to the whole of
nature. However before long there was a change of another sort,
the fourth of these special acts of God's power which was yet
again due to man's sin.

4. *The Confusion of Language*.

Genesis 10 & 11 show that the survivors of the Flood quickly
multiplied, and they came to Babel in the land of Shinar
(Gen.11.2). This was at, or near, Babylon, the city later made

famous by Nebuchadnezzar (Dan.1.2). This is in one of the most fertile regions of the world in an area watered by the rivers Euphrates and Tigris which rise in the mountains of Ararat and flow down to the Persian Gulf.   At Babel they decided to build 'a city and a tower whose top *may reach* unto heaven' (Gen.11.4). Their motives for doing this were evidently very wrong; it seems to have been done in pride and in defiance of God. In pride they wanted to make for themselves 'a name' (Gen.11.4); in defiance of God they did not want to be 'scattered abroad upon the face of the whole earth' (Gen.11.4), which would have been necessary to carry out God's command to 'replenish the earth' after the worldwide flood (Gen.9.1). Possibly, not believing God's promise, they also imagined that by building such a high tower they could escape another flood, or even by reaching to heaven make themselves as God. Extensive findings in the region by archaeologists also suggest that the tower may have been intended for idolatrous worship of the moon and stars; this may be why the words in italics in Gen.11.4 were not in the original. Babylonian legend attributes the building to Nimrod who, the Bible tells us, founded a kingdom here (Gen.10.9,10).

God therefore determined to intervene and put a stop to this work and compel the people to spread over the earth and replenish it. The way He did this was to 'confound their language that they may not understand one another's speech. So the Lord scattered them abroad from thence upon the face of all the earth' (Gen.11.7,8). There was, it seems, only one language in the world until then but when God intervened men suddenly found that their languages were different and they could not understand each other. Because they could not communicate properly they could not work together; those who did have a common language, possibly families or tribes, formed groups which moved off in different directions to 'replenish the earth'. To begin with they went to adjacent countries as indicated in

Gen.10; the record in that chapter agrees well with later parts of the Bible and with what is known from archaeology; Asshur, for example, founded Assyria with its capital at Nineveh (Gen.10.11).

The modern world has inherited this curse of Babel, and what a curse it is! What God does He does perfectly and He certainly confounded human language perfectly. The trouble has been further compounded because, as languages alter with time, many more languages have developed from those which were created at Babel. There are now in the region of 6000 languages; many of them are related but there are at least fifty different groups of languages which bear no relationship to each other. Although anthropologists now generally recognise the unity of the human race, no one can find a relationship between these diverse groups. There is no satisfactory explanation for this other than the one given in the Bible; moreover the more complex languages do not appear to have developed from simpler ones, as the theory of evolution would suggest, but rather the older languages often tend to be more complex.

This last of God's special acts evidently took place fairly soon after the Flood; possibly Gen.10.25 indicates that it was about the time that Peleg was born which was 101 years after the Flood (Gen.11.10-17). Starting from the information in Gen.11.10-26 it was deduced by Bishop Ussher that the Flood took place about 4500 years ago; his calculation may not be completely accurate, but it is clear that any date very much earlier than this could not be consistent with the Bible record. Many more changes have taken place during this period and some of these have made and are making the world still less like the original paradise. These changes may well have included further widespread catastrophes but there is no indication of any further acts of God with such universal results.

CHAPTER 2

POPULAR THEORIES OF ORIGINS

Over the years there have been many theories advanced by unbelieving scientists to account for the origin of the world and life; different theories have grown and declined in popularity and such theories are still frequently modified in the light of new discoveries. Today the most popular account includes:

– the development of everything in the universe in accordance with what is known as the 'principle of uniformity';

– an original 'Big Bang' leading to the formation of the entire universe;

– the appearance of an elementary form of life by chance;

– the progressive development from this, in accordance with the theory of evolution, of all forms of life;

– the gradual deposition of layers of rocks on the earth's surface by currently known processes;

– an immense age for the universe.

A simple outline of each of these elements is given below.

1. *The Principle of Uniformity.*

According to this principle everything has come about solely by the operation of the present laws of nature, through processes and causes which can be observed today, and therefore without the intervention of God; this principle is the fundamental assumption underlying all the popular theories. In its simplest form it supposes that natural processes have always been taking place at the same rate; for example, if a stalactite 50 cm. long is known to have grown 1 cm. in the last 200 years then on this

14

assumption each 1 cm. of its length would have taken the same time to grow, giving it an age of 200 x 50 = 10,000 years other things being equal. This principle is generally true of created things, as might be expected in an orderly creation, and it is a very important basis of true science. In the theories which are generally taught today, however, its application is extended to try to explain creation and other events which the Bible attributes to God's special acts.

Until quite recently because of this principle its supporters have supposed that changes through the ages have been gradual, since that is what is generally seen today; any suggestion that some changes occurred as a result of a worldwide catastrophe was usually dismissed as unscientific. More recently the accumulation of evidence has convinced many scientists that there must indeed have been one or more global catastrophes. They consider that only cataclysmic events could account for some geological features and the mass extinction of living creatures, such as dinosaurs, to which the fossils bear witness. The nature of such events is the subject of much speculation; the 'asteroid impact' theory is quite popular at present. This suggests that the earth collided with an extra-terrestrial object, such as a comet, asteroid or meteorite large enough to cause major changes in climate, geography, geology and natural life. It has been suggested that the impact was in the Pacific Ocean area with an energy perhaps 10,000 times greater than that of the world's entire stock of nuclear weapons.

2. *The 'Big Bang' Theory.*

The rainbow is the result of the separation of the light from the sun into different colours by drops of water; a finer separation can be obtained by optical equipment, using the same principle, and this shows that there are many separate coloured components in the 'spectrum' each with its own frequency. Light from distant galaxies contains many of the same components but their frequencies appear to be slightly lower; they have been shifted towards the red end of the spectrum. This is thought to be due to the 'Döppler' effect; this effect is more commonly observed in the apparent change in the note of the siren of a passing police car; the sound waves are compressed when it is approaching giving a higher pitch but when it is receding the sound waves are extended, lowering the pitch. Because the shift towards red is equivalent to lowering the pitch, it is believed that most of the galaxies are receding rapidly and therefore the universe is expanding. If it has always been expanding it would have been concentrated at a single point at some time in the very distant past. The 'Big Bang' theory supposes that at this point there was an event, likened to an immense explosion, from which proceeded all the energy and basic matter for the entire universe. From this moment, at least, the principle of uniformity is assumed to have operated. At first the energy was so concentrated and the temperature so high that it could not be described in terms of components which are familiar today; as this nucleus expanded it began to cool and form particles then gases which subsequently condensed to form galaxies and stars.

The theory of what caused the 'Big Bang' is less well developed. Some, apparently including a recent pope, feel it is appropriate to attribute this to a divine creator; others, not wishing to have a place for any creator in their scheme, suggest that the universe never had a beginning. One idea is that the 'Big Bang' resulted from the sudden chance combination of chaotic gravitational fields which previously existed, another is that it resulted from the collapse of a previously existing universe.

3. *Chance Origin of Life*.

This is the theory that, after the earth solidified and cooled, atoms and simple molecules came together, by chance, to form some of the basic complex molecules on which life depends. By the same chance process some of these molecules combined in such a way that the resulting structure was able to reproduce itself and formed the first single-celled living organism. Ability to reproduce is an essential feature of all known life.

It is supposed that life first appeared in this way in a fluid environment containing a mixture of appropriate organic compounds and other ingredients, sometimes referred to as a 'primaeval soup'. This theory depends, amongst other things, on the assumption that there was no oxygen in the earth's atmosphere in those days.

4. *The Theory of Evolution.*

It is well known that variations occur within families of living creatures. By selective breeding, particular characteristics of colour, size and shape can be developed, for example, in roses and dogs. Charles Darwin saw, in the early nineteenth century, that some variations of this kind occurred naturally in wild creatures, such as the finches he studied, and that those variants most suited to their particular environment flourished. From this Darwin proposed a general theory of evolution, based on the principle of uniformity, to account for the origin of the species. According to this theory there is no limit to the extent of variations possible given sufficient time, and these variations alone have accounted for all the changes from the first living cells to the whole of the known modern forms of life. Small variations occurred and the most successful or fittest variants survived by 'natural selection'. This process continued through numerous generations over extremely long periods of time until many small variations accumulated into large changes. Many-celled creatures evolved, backbones and sight developed, fishes appeared, then reptiles, birds, mammals and eventually man. Family trees or 'evolutionary series' have been drawn up showing the sequence in which the 'higher order' creatures are assumed to have evolved from earlier, 'lower order' ones.

The theory has been altered substantially from time to time to make it compatible with more recent findings. It is now known that the 'genes' of each cell contain the information (comparable to computer 'software') which determines how a cell will function, multiply and grow into a fully developed organism, with its own individual characteristics. Disorganising agents such as some forms of radiation can give rise to 'mutations' by penetrating cells and modifying the genes; when this happens in reproductive cells the offspring may differ from the parent. More recent evolutionary theory has concentrated on variations arising from mutations in the genes.

5. *The Formation of Rocks.*

About three-quarters of the rocks in the earth's surface, including many at the tops of mountains, are 'sedimentary'. They appear to have been produced when material, suspended in water, was deposited forming layers or 'strata'; the strata in such rocks may often be seen clearly in the cliffs at the seaside. The popular theory assumes that these strata have been laid down gradually, one upon another in accordance with the principle of uniformity, by processes such as silting which can be observed today. The age of rocks is estimated on the basis of these assumptions and those of the theory of evolution.

According to the theory of evolution the 'simple' forms of life came first followed by progressively more complex forms; thus the simpler forms should be found in the strata which are older, and therefore deeper in the earth, and the more complex forms in the younger, higher strata. On this basis a systematic table, or 'geological column' was drawn up, with the oldest rocks at the bottom of the column and the youngest at the top. The column was divided into named 'eras', 'periods' and 'epochs' (such as 'Mesozoic', 'Jurassic' and 'Pliocene'); each of these is associated with the characteristic or 'index' fossils of its particular time. A sedimentary rock is said to belong to the division of geological time appropriate to the index fossils it contains, regardless of the nature of the rock itself and its depth in the earth. This column is used as the standard rock sequence worldwide; it has been unchanged in its main outline since before 1840.

6. *The Vast Age of the Universe.*

If these theories are correct it must have taken an extremely long time for the universe to reach its present state, whichever field of study is considered:

– Astronomy suggests that at today's apparent rate of expansion it would have taken about 15 billion (thousand million) years for the universe to reach its present size if it started from a single point. Astronomy also suggests that light or radio signals reaching the earth from the most distant known objects have taken billions of years for their journey. If the principle of uniformity alone has always applied then these objects must have existed for at least this length of time.

– Geology suggests that it would have taken hundreds of millions of years for the sedimentary rocks to have been deposited at rates which can be observed today. The sedimentary chalk of Dunstable Downs which is 120 metres thick is said to have been deposited by a prehistoric sea over a period of 12 million years. Some sedimentary deposits are several miles thick.

– Biology can only observe today variations which are minute compared with the total supposed variations from the first simple life. Therefore the total evolutionary process must have taken many millions of times longer than any observed change.

The age of the earth itself is generally put at about 4500 million years.

The validity of these popular theories is usually taken for granted; they are often taught as facts or even claimed to have been proved scientifically. This is not true; the original processes involved in creation cannot be observed nor can theories about them be tested in the way that other scientific theories can be. However firmly they may be believed by their supporters they can only be theories. Objections to these theories, and the existence of serious alternatives to them, are at best rarely mentioned and at worst actively suppressed.

CHAPTER 3

OBJECTIONS TO THE POPULAR THEORIES

The overriding objection to the popular theories reviewed in the previous chapter is that they ignore, and are in many respects contrary to, the word of God. The Bible clearly teaches that, in addition to the general operation of the laws of nature, there were the special acts of God which took place a few thousand years ago. The popular theories attempt to replace these special acts with the operations of the principle of uniformity over many millions of years.

There is also a case against these popular theories on general and scientific grounds. A simple outline of this case is given in this chapter.

1. *Evolution not demonstrated.*

No new type of creature has ever been observed to have evolved from existing creatures. There is a great deal of variation in such characteristics as shape, size and colour between individuals or groups within a 'kind', but there is an apparent limit to the amount of variation which even controlled breeding can produce; this limit is set by the range of variation present in the ancestral genes of the particular 'kind'. Other changes can occur by mutations, but the genetic structure is so complex and finely balanced that such changes are almost invariably harmful. An accidental change to any complex system, such as a large computer programme, can be expected to cause it to operate imperfectly if at all, not to improve it. So it is with living organisms; variations due to mutations do not produce successful new 'kinds'. Scientists have bred more than a thousand generations of fruit-fly (drosophila); these insects have been subjected to X-rays and other agents to increase the number of mutations but, although this has produced many variants, no new species have resulted. No experiment or observation has even identified a new functioning organ. Cross breeding between different 'kinds' has been demonstrated but any resulting hybrids are invariably infertile; the mule is a well known example of this. It may be argued that scientists have not yet had enough time to observe or demonstrate the development of new organs and new species; if, however, all the living species have evolved from a primary single cell in the past 600 million years, the appearance of new species and new organs must have been a relatively common occurrence.

'Natural selection', unlike evolution, can be observed. However it does not lead to evolution but rather to conservation; it enables organisms to adapt, within limits, to survive and it tends to eliminate mutations.

2. *Evolution contrary to basic natural and scientific law.*

In nature, and in other spheres, chaos replaces organisation in systems which are left to themselves. Living things revert to the wild forms if left alone, they do not develop unaided into more advanced forms. Higher forms of energy, such as radioactivity, degrade into lower forms of heat energy while the complex elements involved, such as radium, change into simpler elements, such as lead. These are all manifestations of a basic scientific principle known as the second law of thermodynamics. The theory of evolution appears to defy this law.

3. *Evolution not supported by the fossil record.*

Fossils are the only certain evidence of the creatures which existed before recorded history and provide the basic data used to justify the theory of evolution. The evolutionary series which have been constructed from the fossil record are, however, purely conjectural; they are based on the assumption that evolutionary theory must be true and the fossils are arranged arbitrarily in the sequence which appears to fit that assumption best. Far from proving the theory the fossil record throws considerable doubt on it.

Gaps in the fossil record.

There are immense gaps in the fossil record in critical places at the very beginning and between the various links in the evolutionary chain:

– Firstly there is no known existing or fossilised form of really simple life. Living things are made up of cells; the simplest known creature past or present consists of a single cell. There is immense complexity in a single cell (see Appendix A) which could not have evolved in one step from inanimate material, yet there is no convincing evidence of simpler life ever having existed.

– Secondly there is a gap in the fossil record between single-celled creatures and those with 800 or more cells. Most of the evidence for the early part of the supposed evolutionary tree is entirely missing: the fossils of very many forms of marine life appear suddenly in rocks which are attributed to a particular period (the 'Cambrian'). All of these forms are quite distinct and fully developed. Very little evidence of life has been found in 'earlier' rocks although evolutionary theory would require a long period of evolutionary development prior to the early Cambrian creatures.

– Thirdly there is no reliable evidence in the fossils of intermediate or transitional forms of life between one 'kind' and another. Claims to have found such evidence are relatively few and there are valid doubts about most of these. For example limbed creatures were supposed to have evolved from fish; the coelacanth fossils were once thought to

23

demonstrate a fish developing limbs but, now that live specimens have been observed in action, the fins are seen to be purely fins, brilliantly designed to allow the fish to swim in every direction. Again, birds were supposed to have evolved from reptiles; the classic example of a possible intermediate form was the archaeopteryx; this has now been shown to be a fully developed, though rather unusual, bird; it has also been shown that feathers develop from an entirely different part of the embryo to that which gives rise to scales in reptiles; moreover quite recently fossils of fully developed birds have been found which are thought to pre-date archaeopteryx. Mammals are also said to have evolved from reptiles; there are 32 orders of mammals, but the earliest and most primitive known members of every order already demonstrate the essential characteristics of the order fully developed. For instance, the earliest known fossil bats are virtually identical with a modern bat. Most of the supposed 'missing links' between apes and men are either the result of inferences drawn from a few bones or can be shown to be apes or men and not transitional forms; at least one well-known example, the Piltdown man, has been shown to be fraudulent. Darwin predicted that, if his theory were true, large numbers of fossils of many intermediate forms would be discovered; this has not happened in spite of intensive search over the past hundred years or so.

– Fourthly the fossil record of insects does not support the theory of evolution. Insects are in some respects the most successful form of life; they exist in every known land and freshwater habitat from desert to arctic and, unlike most other members of the animal kingdom, successfully resist all man's attempts to exterminate them. They are designed quite differently from other creatures and there is no fossil evidence of evolutionary ancestors or descendants; all known insect fossils are fully developed varieties of types known today.

– Fifthly, there is no real evidence in the fossils of plant evolution. Numerous fossilised plants found in 'early' strata are identical to those growing today. As with animal life many species have become extinct but this does not make them ancestors of modern plants.

Sequence of fossil record in doubt.

There is also much evidence in the fossil record which throws doubt on the sequence and timing of the supposed developments in the evolutionary series:

– Many ancient fossils have been found which are identical to today's species and which in no way represent primitive ancestors. Living creatures have been found in recent times which were only previously known as fossils. For example, the coelacanth already referred to, was assumed to have been extinct for about 60 million years as no younger fossils had been found. In these cases, at least, ancient and modern life forms are found to be contemporary, not separated by millions of years of evolutionary development. The fossil record does show that large numbers of prehistoric creatures have become extinct but this does not prove that they were links in an evolutionary chain. Many creatures are becoming extinct today but this is due particularly to pressure from mankind and not to any evolutionary process. It has been forecast that a million species of life will be lost in the next 25 years.

– The supposed evolutionary progression from 'lower' to 'higher' forms of life is the basis for the geological column described in chapter 2 (5). Whilst there is, in many places, some order in the sequence of rock strata, the geological column does not actually exist anywhere in the real world. In any one place only a few of the many periods are represented and these are sometimes in the wrong order with the 'older' fossils on top of 'younger' ones. This effect is usually explained as the result of rock movements; there is, however, no known process taking place today which could account for thousands of square miles of rock having been moved sideways for many miles. It is even doubtful whether the rocks themselves could withstand the forces necessary to accomplish such movements. Sometimes the most recent rocks are found in direct contact with the very oldest with no apparent evidence that they were not deposited that way originally.

'Circular reasoning'.

The dating of rocks by the index fossils and the dating of fossils by the rocks has been described as 'circular reasoning'. It can only be valid if the evolutionary assumptions are valid; it cannot prove any of the theories. In any case fossils are sometimes found in strata of the 'wrong' period.

4. *'Vestigial' organs no evidence of evolution.*

The human body contains about 180 organs, such as the appendix, which may not appear to be essential. These were thought by evolutionists to be the relics of organs which were required by the earlier forms of life from which man was supposed to have descended. With the advance of medical knowledge, however, the function of all but 6 of these organs can now be explained. Similarly there was a theory that during the period from conception to birth the human embryo goes through stages which repeat evolutionary history; for example at one stage of its development the embryo was said to exhibit fish-like gills. These ideas can also be refuted by means of modern medical knowledge.

5. *Uniformity cannot explain the evidence.*

The principle of uniformity cannot satisfactorily explain observed factual evidence which supports the biblical position that the earth is a few thousand years old. On the other hand observed evidence which supports the old earth theory can generally be accounted for in the light of the alternative biblical creation based theories advanced in the next chapter. Appendix B summarises the evidence on the age of the earth, and its interpretation.

Apart from this fundamental issue, fossilisation and many of the world's rock structures cannot be satisfactorily explained on the basis of the principle of uniformity:

– When animals and plants die today they do not normally fossilise, they decompose and disintegrate. At the time when many of the sedimentary rocks were laid down, however, fossilisation must have occurred on a massive scale and the fossils, in general, show no sign of decomposition. For large animals to be preserved in this way thick layers of sediment must have been deposited very much more quickly than happens today. Coal and oil are the products of fossilisation; most experts acknowledge that these are not generally being formed today. Thus processes observable today do not account for the past as far as the mass of fossils are concerned.

– Many of the earth's existing rock formations must have arisen from geologic processes which were different both in nature and degree from those which are observable today. Volcanic activity of the type and extent experienced in recent times could not account for many of the volcanic formations and lava fields which exist. The great mountain chains appear to have been lifted up from the sea bottom in comparatively recent geologic periods but no satisfactory, generally accepted, theory exists for this. The study of sedimentary rocks shows that the deposition processes of the past must also have differed in quality and quantity from those of today. Uniformity cannot adequately explain, for example, the geology of the Grand

Canyon area as will be seen in chapter 4 (4).

6. *Evolution a virtual mathematical impossibility.*

Scientists have discovered the structure of many of the tremendously complex biochemical molecules which are essential to life. From this knowledge it is possible to make a mathematical calculation of the probability that these molecules could form by chance. It is also possible to work out the probability of particular biochemicals, such as the enzymes, occurring in the right combinations; a vast number of combinations might exist but only precisely correct ones are viable. Then again probabilities can be calculated of chance mutations leading to particular proteins in, for example, a gorilla being changed to the corresponding ones in man.

Calculations of this kind result in such exceedingly low probabilities that evolution can be said to be a virtual mathematical impossibility, even in the many millions of years postulated by evolutionary scientists for the age of the earth. Various comparisons have been made to try to illustrate this conclusion. The number of grains of sand in the world and the number of atoms in the entire universe are thought to be tiny numbers compared with the calculated odds against some of these biochemical events occurring by chance. This is a most powerful scientific argument for rejecting the theory of evolution and because of its importance a simplified outline of some key aspects of the chemistry of life is given in Appendix A.

7. *The General Credibility Problem with Evolution.*

A non-mathematical way of expressing doubts like those in the previous section would be to say that there is a serious general credibility problem with evolution. These doubts apply to the larger scale features of life as much as to biochemistry. None of the marvels of modern technology would be possible without the efforts of brilliant scientists, engineers and designers; by the same token countless features of life seem, to many people, to demonstrate a design capability far exceeding present human endeavours. Even popular books based on evolution use such expressions as 'the miracle of nature' to describe the powers of sight and flight, and then claim that the eye evolved from nothing and feathers evolved from reptiles' scales, which are totally different structures.

Although these theories are widely accepted and taught there are, and always have been, scientists who doubted them. Some of these accept them, albeit with misgivings, because they represent the views of the scientific establishment, some because the alternative of divine creation is to them unthinkable. Increasing numbers of scientists are rejecting these theories on purely scientific grounds; generally without having anything to offer in their place, although a few postulate fanciful alternatives. There is however a significant but relatively small minority of scientists who are believers; some of these have done a good deal of work in comparatively recent years to show how the discoveries of science might be interpreted in the light of the Holy Scriptures. The next chapter outlines some of their conclusions.

CHAPTER 4

BIBLE-BASED SCIENTIFIC THEORIES

The purpose of this chapter is to demonstrate that there are theories of origins, which are themselves scientific, and which are consistent both with the facts given in the Bible and the factual observations of science today.

The account most widely proposed by Bible believing scientists includes:

– the whole biblical record as reviewed in chapter 1 with its implication of a relatively young earth;

– the consequent belief that all the world's genetic material was created at the outset;

– the theory that the 'waters above the firmament' consisted of a huge water vapour canopy round the earth which collapsed as part of the Flood;

– the theory that vast underground water systems fed the rivers in the original creation and that these were broken up as part of the Flood;

– the theory that the origin of many of the sedimentary rocks, fossils and high mountain ranges was associated with the Flood.

An outline of these theories and their consequential implications, together with some of the biblical and scientific evidence to support them, is given in the sections which follow. The term 'creationist' is used to distinguish these theories from the 'popular' and 'evolutionary' theories of chapter 2.

1. *Creation and the Origin of Life.*

The earth's design is ideally suited for the life on it. It has just
the right size, composition, gravity, atmosphere, rate of rotation,
distance from the sun, period of rotation around the sun, to
mention a few of its characteristics. These are all finely balanced
within quite narrow limits so that a relatively small change would
make the planet uninhabitable, like all the other planets. For
example, it is estimated that it would only need a reduction of
10% in the earth's diameter for it to lose most of its atmosphere,
due to lower gravity. The Voyager space probes have recently
provided a great deal of surprising new information about other
bodies in the solar system; it is now clearer than ever that they
are utterly uninhabitable except possibly in special artificial
environments. The earth is unique in the solar system; it was
perfectly designed and created by God for His intended purpose.

Because creation was a finished work it must have contained
all the 'kinds' of creatures which ever lived. While these would
probably not have exhibited all the variations which have
subsequently arisen, the genes of the original creatures contained
the potential for such variations so that, for example, black, white
and coloured people all descended from Adam. The general
principle applies to vegetation as much as it does to the creatures.
Life multiplied and the earth became filled with abundant,
diverse life until the Flood came.

2. *The Earth before the Flood.*

Some physical changes took place due to the Fall as reviewed in
chapter 1. At this stage the 'waters above the firmament' would
still have been in position although there is nothing apparent
today to answer this description. One of the main creationist
theories suggests that these waters consisted of a huge canopy of
water vapour high up in, or above, the earth's atmosphere. Water
vapour is lighter than air and the upper regions are warm; the

water vapour would remain transparent in the canopy without condensing into clouds or falling as rain provided there were no particles there to provide nuclei for the formation of droplets of condensation.

This canopy would have had some profound effects on the conditions on earth; it would have the following implications for climate, geology , atmospheric pressure and the earth's exposure to radiation:

Climate.

Objects exposed to the sun gain heat from its rays and lose heat by emitting infra-red radiation. The glass of a greenhouse is relatively transparent to the sun's rays coming in but not to infra-red radiation going out; the inside therefore tends to gain heat. The canopy would have acted in the same way. The present 'greenhouse effect' is mainly due to the water vapour, carbon dioxide, methane, ozone and CFC gases in the atmosphere. People are concerned today that a comparatively small increase in this effect would damage the climate and raise the level of the oceans by melting some of the polar ice. The much greater effect of the canopy could well have meant that there was no polar ice at all in the beginning; moreover because of the insulating effect of the canopy there would be comparatively little temperature difference between arctic and tropics, summer and winter, and day and night; conditions would be almost universally 'tropical'. Since the global temperature differences cause the winds and weather there would be no strong winds or rain storms; rather there would be a calm, humid atmosphere permitting abundant, continuous growth of lush vegetation. In keeping with the abundant vegetation there would probably have been more carbon dioxide in the atmosphere; this would have emphasised the greenhouse effect still further.

The Bible gives hints that climatic conditions may indeed have been like this; the following references suggest that it was humid and that possibly rain, clouds, wind and seasons as known today did not exist. Mists and rivers watered the garden of Eden, there was no rain there (Gen.2.5), the first rain mentioned was at the Flood (Gen.7.4); the bow in the clouds appears to have been a new experience to Noah for him to have accepted it as a sign from God (Gen.9.13). It seems to have been harvest time all the year round in the garden of Eden and wind and clouds, seasons, and cold and heat are only mentioned after the Flood (Gen.8.1; 8.22; & 9.13).

Scientific evidence also clearly demonstrates that the earth's climate was just like this for most of the supposed past geological periods; this conclusion is uncontroversial. Global temperatures were higher than today. Fossils of animals and plants are to be found at all latitudes which can now only be found living, if at all, in the warmer regions; for example recent discoveries in Antarctica show that even there plant life once thrived in a moist, warm climate. Lush vegetation provided a plentiful food supply for abundant animal life all over the world. Types of plant, such as those which later became coal, show that the climate in widespread regions of the world must have been very warm and humid all year round.

There may have been another factor partly responsible for the relative absence of seasons before the Flood: the earth's axis may not have been so tilted as it is today. This creationist theory is based on a scientific study of the history of the earth's tilt; this suggests that there may have been a major disturbance at a date close to that of the Flood. This could be explained by an event such as that in the asteroid impact theory referred to in chapter 2.

Geology.

'A river went out of Eden to water the garden; and from thence it was parted, and became into four heads' (Gen.2.10);

one of them compassed 'the whole land of Ethiopia' and another was Euphrates (Gen.2.13,14), so they must have been substantial rivers. But there was no rain (Gen.2.5), so where did the rivers come from? A creationist theory is that there were extensive underground systems containing water under pressure and the rivers were fed from these systems through something like artesian springs. Water and oil are found under pressure within the earth's crust today, but these systems must have been on a much larger scale.

It will be seen in section 3 of this chapter that before the Flood the geological structure of the earth's crust was very different from what it is now; most of the sedimentary rocks probably did not then exist and perhaps there were no high mountains. If there were few sedimentary rocks there would necessarily have been few fossils.

This theory is consistent with the biblical record and relevant scientific observations such as the following:

– geologists generally agree that the high mountain ranges are constructed from some of the youngest rocks in the world, and there is plenty of evidence that many of them were once under water;

– much of the earth's water is said to be volcanic in origin and therefore came in some way from within the earth;

– the fossils appear suddenly at a particular period in the rocks; 'older' rocks are largely devoid of fossils.

Atmospheric pressure.

Atmospheric or barometric pressure is due to the weight of the atmosphere; the canopy, unless it were in orbit, would add to this pressure.

There is evidence to suggest that higher pressures are

beneficial, given the same oxygen content of the air; since the original creation was perfect no doubt the original atmospheric pressure and content would have been ideal.

Radiation.

The earth today is subjected to many powerful radiations from outside; these are partially filtered out by the atmosphere but a water vapour canopy would be a much more effective shield. These radiations tend to cause harmful mutations and are believed to have caused damage to man's genetic system. Another effect of cosmic radiation is that it turns some of the nitrogen in the air into radioactive carbon (Carbon 14). As carbon is the basic element of all life, all living things absorb a proportion of radiocarbon; when a living thing dies the radioactivity from this carbon begins to decay and decreases to half its original level in about 6000 years. The level of radioactivity in dead material can therefore be used to estimate the date of death; this method has proved to be reasonably reliable for ages of up to about 3000 years. Before the Flood there would have been very little radiocarbon because of the screening effect of the canopy. Fossils of organisms which died during or before the Flood would therefore exhibit an extremely low level of radioactivity. This is exactly what is found in practice. Evolutionists, ignoring the Flood, interpret the low radioactivity as proving that the fossils are very old.

3. *The Flood.*

The Flood was not caused by atmospheric and underground supplies of water ('rains' and 'fountains') as known today; these could only provide a small fraction of the volume of water needed to cover all the mountains, even though these may have been lower than they are now. The water in the canopy and the underground systems, on the other hand, could well have been sufficient to flood the earth to this extent. The cause of this great cataclysm was undoubtedly divine power; this may have been through the voice of God as in creation, speaking and it was done, or it may have been through providential overruling of natural events and processes. The fountains of the great deep may have been broken up by geological action akin to volcanic or earthquake activity but on a larger scale than anything known to history, or, it could have been due to the impact of an asteroid or other external body. The tilt in the earth's axis, already referred to, and the reported existence of an iridium layer in the rocks in many places may be the results of such an event. Any of these causes could also have led to the collapse of the water vapour canopy. Volcanic explosions in recent times have given rise to immense dust clouds high up in the atmosphere; this kind of effect, or meteoric dust or the tail of a comet could have provided the particles needed as nuclei for the water vapour to condense.

The waters covered the mountains for months before they abated to reveal dry land again. The canopy and the fountains of the great deep were not restored as far as is known and evaporation could only account for a small part of the water level reduction, perhaps 5cm. Creationists have suggested that the waters went down because, in the continuation of the geological upheaval, the mountains were raised to something like their present heights and the valleys in the sea were deepened. This idea may be supported by Psa.104.6-9: 'the waters stood above the mountains' (v.6) 'at the voice of thy thunder they hasted away' (v.7) 'the mountains ascend, the valleys descend' (v.8 margin). There is also scientific evidence for this possibility; firstly it is generally thought that many of the high mountain ranges are 'young' and were once beneath the sea; secondly the quantity of water in the oceans seems about right for this explanation. The highest point on the land is about 5 miles above and the lowest point in the sea is about 7 miles below sea level. If there were no valleys in the sea or mountains on the land it is estimated that there is enough water today to cover the world to a depth of about 2 miles; this would be enough to deluge the earth if the mountains were relatively low and the seas more shallow.

Billions of land creatures perished in the Flood; many of these were quickly buried in the sediment and became fossilised. Fossils are found in great 'graveyards' in many places in the world each containing millions of fossils; many fossils indicate that the creatures were in good condition, and many show evidence of sudden death. It is claimed that most of the dinosaur fossils show that they died by drowning.

The fossils also include those of marine creatures; myriads of these also perished in the general destruction. Some were swept away and enveloped in the solid matter carried by the flood waters, others may have died due to such effects as the lack of oxygen in water churned up from the depths. Whilst some species of marine creature might have become extinct as a result, many survived; the Bible only refers to total destruction of the creatures of the dry land (Gen.7.21-23).

Vegetation suffered in much the same way. Coal and oil are the products of fossilisation. Coal is a type of sedimentary rock formed when the giant fern-like trees which grew in lush, swampy forests were buried at considerable depths under great pressure. Coal is found in many different parts of the world. Oil was formed from masses of plankton-like creatures under great pressure. It is almost universally agreed that conditions today are not generally suitable for the formation of significant quantities of fossils, coal or oil.

Many of the sedimentary rocks, which form 75% of the earth's surface today, are considered to be a direct consequence of the Flood. The turbulent waters of the Flood would have carried with them immense quantities of soil and rock and, as the sea still does, would have ground much of this material into particles of various sizes. The material would have been deposited as the waters became less turbulent; different currents at different speeds from various directions would have tended to deposit the material in layers, or strata, of different types of material and different particle size. This property of moving water to sort material in this way is used today; the Cornish tin mines used it very effectively to separate the tin oxide from the stone particles in crushed ore. The sedimentary deposits would subsequently have compacted under their own weight and dried out; later movements and erosion have modified these formations to give the strata which can be seen today. Some sedimentary rocks, and other geological changes, may well be due to other widespread catastrophic events of which the Bible says nothing, but never again was there total destruction of life.

There is a measure of order about the sequence of the rock strata, and the deposition of the fossils; in practice this order is not as systematic as in the idealised form of the geological column described in chapter 2. Evolutionists, ignoring the Flood, consider that the more deeply buried fossils are millions of years older than those nearer the surface. Creationists believe that a large proportion of the fossils had their origin in the Flood and that the order which does exist can be attributed to factors such as the following:

– the process of sorting of particles described above;

– different types of layer resulting from different phases of the Flood;

– the possibility that other catastrophes were responsible for some of the rocks and fossils;

– the order in which living creatures would have been affected by the Flood. The creatures of the deep sea bottoms would be overwhelmed or poisoned by the breaking up of the fountains of the great deep, then fish nearer the surface would have been overcome by materials washing down from the

land. Larger animals and men would in many cases have been
able to take refuge on higher ground and so be among the last
to have perished.

The many exceptions found to the general sequence of fossils
can be readily understood if this is the correct explanation of their
origin. These theories can also account for the very existence
and nature of the fossils. Animals and plants must be buried
quickly if they are to fossilise rather than decompose. Large
animal fossils and fossilised tree trunks extending through
several strata up to about 3 metres thick are fairly common; this
indicates that these strata were all deposited at about the same
time, not gradually over millions of years.

4. *The Earth after the Flood.*

The main features of the present earth emerged after the Flood.
Climate, geography and geology and life itself had been radically
affected:

Climate.

Climatic conditions after the Flood were much harsher and
more variable. With the loss of the major part of the greenhouse
effect and the possible tilt in the earth's axis the climate
eventually settled into the general pattern of temperature
differences, wind, weather and seasons known today. Before
conditions stabilised there would probably have been some drastic
temporary effects, in particular there may have been a sudden
'freeze-up' affecting large parts of the world. This could have
been caused by the rapid loss of the greenhouse effect and may
have been made worse by the sun being obscured, either by the
dust clouds resulting from geological upheaval or by ice-crystal
clouds which might have resulted from an asteroid impact. It is
thought that there would be a big freeze-up after a nuclear war for
some of the same reasons. Only a severe, sudden freeze-up could

account for the five million or so frozen mammoths which exist in Siberia and Alaska; a few of these are whole, most are torn to pieces showing signs of sudden death followed by rapid freezing. There are many other animals found like this, from sheep to tigers, in these regions.

Although many aspects of the subject are controversial it is generally accepted that the evidence points to there having been one or more 'ice ages'. Numerous imaginative theories have been proposed for their origin but it could well be that the main cause was these after effects of the Flood. As conditions settled and vegetation again multiplied on earth greenhouse gases would have built up somewhat and reached a measure of stability at a new level; some warming would have occurred leaving the ice confined to the polar regions.

Geography and geology.

Geographical features had been drastically changed and continents, mountain ranges, oceans and rivers would also have settled eventually into something similar to the present pattern. There have been further changes and these are continuing: islands are being formed, the sea is encroaching in places and sediment is still being deposited but none of these are on a scale which is comparable to the transformation caused by the Flood.

As with the climate there would probably have been some further significant changes before things stabilised. The sedimentary rocks would have been soft and easily eroded; this could explain such spectacular effects as the Grand Canyon where a 3 mile gorge has been cut through sedimentary rocks a mile deep. Popular theories attribute canyons like this to a repeated process of uplift and erosion over millions of years. If this were the true cause it is most unlikely that the strata would have remained horizontal over an area of about 250,000 square miles, and that the canyons would meander as many of them do;

meandering only occurs where banks are soft, as they would have been shortly after the Flood when there would still have been fairly heavy currents of water flowing.

Life.

The harsher and more seasonal climatic conditions did not permit the return of such extensive, lush vegetation as existed previously; this would imply a much reduced food supply in many parts of the world. This together with colder and more variable climatic conditions would have seriously affected the survival of many species; some would only be able to survive in tropical regions whilst large, cold blooded animals requiring huge supplies of food and an even temperature may have been unable to survive even in the tropics. Only two of each kind (other than 'clean beasts') were saved in the ark so any one death immediately after the Flood could have led to the extinction of that sort of creature.

It is no surprise therefore that the fossils include those of many species which have been extinct throughout recorded history. Perhaps the best known and most spectacular examples are the dinosaurs; many other giant variants as well as many smaller creatures found in fossilised form are also unknown to recorded history. As already indicated in chapter 2 (1) the mass extinction of so many species, apparently at about the same period of time, is so remarkable that many evolutionists now recognise that it cannot be explained on the basis of uniformity.

Men's lives became shorter. Before the Flood men lived for about 900 years (Gen.5) but by the time of Moses the normal life span was reckoned as 70 years (Psa.90.10). This reduction was no doubt divinely overruled, but natural processes largely resulting from the Flood may have been important contributory factors. Genetic degeneration, possibly caused by the cumulative effects of cosmic radiation in successive generations since the

41

Flood may be one factor; reduced barometric pressure could have been another. Disease and the harsher conditions may also have been involved in the process.

In concluding this summary of creationist theories it must be stressed that however satisfactory and convincing they may appear to be to some believers, what is not directly recorded in the Bible or cannot be observed today is still only theory. These theories are no more capable of scientific proof than the evolutionary theories; it must moreover be appreciated that the subject is so complex and human knowledge so limited that no theory can be expected to explain everything in detail.

CHAPTER 5

THE FUTURE

As there are two fundamentally different beliefs about the beginning of the world and the origin of life so there are equally different expectations concerning the future. Evolutionists discount the biblical record of the special acts of God in the beginning and by the same token they discount the Bible prophecies of the way God will bring this world to an end.

1. *The popular theories.*

Application of the principle of uniformity, without allowing for God's intervention, leads to the expectation of major changes taking place over exceedingly long periods of time, as supposedly happened in the past:

– Evolution would presumably continue with life developing into ever more advanced forms. If evolution achieved so much in the past surely there would be no limit to what wonders it might accomplish in the future; even so there seem to be very few serious suggestions as to what advances might be expected.

– Another possible gradual change is foreseen within the solar system; as the sun loses energy and cools down it might gradually expand to become a 'red giant' star which would eventually swallow the earth.

– The universe might or might not continue to expand indefinitely. If the total quantity, or 'mass', of material in the universe is less than a certain critical value, expansion would continue; matter would eventually be infinitely thinly spread out in space, the stars would burn out their energy and all would become cold and dark. If, on the other hand, the total mass of material in the universe is greater than the critical value, the force of gravity would prevail in the long run; expansion would slow down and be followed by contraction. If this were to occur the universe could ultimately collapse back to a single point perhaps even leading to another 'Big Bang'! The observable mass of material in the universe is less than the critical value but many scientists now consider that there may be sufficient unobservable matter, for example in 'black holes', to cause contraction to take place in due course. Either way the future timescales involved would be greater than the supposed 10 to 20 billion years since the original 'Big Bang'.

2. *The Bible*.

Holy Scripture clearly prophesies that the world will not continue indefinitely. God will intervene the fourth time because of sin; as in the days of Noah 'evil men ... shall wax worse and worse' (2 Tim.3.13) and then as the old world 'being overflowed with water, perished' so 'the heavens and the earth, which are now, by the same word are kept in store, reserved unto fire against the day of judgment and perdition of ungodly men .... The day of the Lord will come as a thief in the night; in the which the heavens shall pass away with a great noise, and the elements shall melt with fervent heat, the earth also and the works that are therein shall be burned up.' (2 Peter 3.6-12). The world's cup of iniquity will finally be full and God will bring this present world to a sudden end.

There are numerous other prophecies of the end of the world:

– The Psalmist says: 'of old hast thou laid the foundation of the earth: and the heavens are the work of thy hands. They shall perish, but thou shalt endure: yea, all of them shall wax old like a garment; as a vesture shalt Thou change them, and they shall be changed' (Psa.102.25,26). This is quoted again in Heb.1.10-12.

– Isaiah records God's words: 'the heavens shall vanish away like smoke, and the earth shall wax old like a garment, and they that dwell therein shall die in like manner' (Isa.51.6).

– Haggai states: 'For thus saith the Lord of hosts; Yet once, it is a little while, and I will shake the heavens, and the earth, and the sea, and the dry land' (Hag.2.6); Hebrews, referring to this shows that it means 'the removing of those things that are shaken' and goes on to say 'for our God is a consuming fire' (Heb.12.26-29).

– Isaiah again prophesies: 'the day of the Lord cometh...For the stars of heaven and the constellations thereof shall not give their light: the sun shall be darkened in his going forth, and the moon shall not cause her light to shine. And I will punish the world for their evil, and the wicked for their iniquity; ... Therefore I will shake the heavens, and the earth shall remove out of her place, in the wrath of the Lord of hosts, and in the day of His fierce anger.' (Isa.13.9-13).

– Jesus quotes and adds to this latter prophecy and makes it clear that 'Heaven and earth shall pass away' and that this will take place suddenly, comparing it to the coming of the Flood, and to the destruction of Sodom (Matt.24.29-39; Luke 17.24-30).

– Jesus prophesies in many other places of His second coming and the end of the world, for example: Matt.13.39; Mark 14.62; Luke 9.26; John 5.28,29.

– Paul speaks repeatedly of it, for example: 1 Cor.15.23,24; 1 Thess.3.13 & 4.16; 2 Thess.1.7-10; 2 Tim.4.1, and the book of the Revelation deals at length with the events at the end of the world.

– Jesus will come again 'in the clouds of heaven with great

power and glory' (Mark.13.26), 'as the lightning' (Matt.24.27) and, as confirmed by the angels , in the same way as He was taken up into heaven at His ascension (Acts1.11).

How long will the world last, when will Jesus come again? Jesus Himself gives the only answer which mankind can have to this question: 'of that day and hour knoweth no man' (Matt.24.36 & 25.13 and elsewhere). Peter, writing of when this day will come, warns that delay in the second coming does not invalidate the prophecies for, says he, 'one day is with the Lord as a thousand years, and a thousand years as one day' (2 Pet.3.8). Jesus warns: 'Watch therefore: for ye know not what hour your Lord doth come ... be ye also ready: for in such an hour as ye think not the Son of man cometh' (Matt.24.42-44 and Luke 12.40). Peter and Paul give similar exhortations to be ready, watching in prayer and soberness. (1 Thess.5.1-6; 1 Pet.4.7).

Although the time is not known there are signs that we are now in the last days. Two references will suffice: 'In the last days ... men shall be lovers of their own selves, covetous, boasters, proud, blasphemers, disobedient to parents, unthankful, unholy, ... lovers of pleasure more than lovers of God; having a form of godliness, but denying the power thereof' (2 Tim.3.1-5); 'Lovers of pleasure more than lovers of God' needs no comment; then how many forms of godliness there are today but how little real religion? At 'the time of the end: many shall run to and fro, and knowledge shall be increased' (Dan.12.4); there has been a tremendous growth in travel, especially in the last thirty years, and the scientific knowledge acquired in the same period in some fields exceeds what was learned in the previous 3000 years! Could anything be more descriptive of the late 20th. century than every word of these sentences?

The difference between the teaching of the Bible and the popular theories is of vital importance to every member of the human race because 'we must all appear before the judgment seat of Christ' (2 Cor.5.10). 'When the Son of man shall come in his glory ... then shall he sit upon the throne of his glory: and before him shall be gathered all nations: and he shall separate them one from another' then each one will hear either 'Come ye blessed of my Father, inherit the kingdom prepared for you from the foundation of the world' or 'Depart from me, ye cursed, into everlasting fire' (Matt.25.31-46). The reality of heaven and hell is testified to in many places in the Bible. The Bible also plainly teaches that 'all have sinned, and come short of the glory of God' (Rom.3.23) and there are none righteous of themselves. Only those who truly believe in Jesus Christ, God's only begotten Son shall 'not perish but have everlasting life' (John 3.16) in the 'new heavens and a new earth wherein dwelleth righteousness' (2 Pet.3.13; see also Isa.65.17 & 66.22 and Rev.21.1 & 27).

Perhaps it is because fallen men do not wish to believe the prophecies of the final judgment that they have devised theories which exclude God. May each one who reads these pages be given grace to heed the exhortation 'Seek ye the Lord while He may be found' (Isa.55.6).

CONCLUSION

This booklet has attempted to show that evolutionary and uniformitarian theories are not based on sound scientific principles but are philosophical hypotheses which could not, in any case, be proven. The Bible clearly shows why such theories are so widely and so fervently believed: because of the Fall, men are spiritually blind and reject God and what the Bible teaches about the power of God and their accountability to their Creator. Some of the many scripture references to this fact include: Job 21.14; Psa.10.4; (see margin especially — 'all his thoughts are, There is no God'); Psa.14.1; Psa.53.1; Rom.1.28; Rom.8.7; 1 Cor.2.14. Peter prophesies specifically that 'there shall come in the last days scoffers . . . saying, Where is the promise of his coming? . . . all things continue as they were from the beginning of the creation. For this they willingly are ignorant of, that by the word of God the heavens were of old, and . . . the world that then was, being overflowed with water, perished'. (2 Pet.3.3-6). In other words he says that they will mock at the prophecy of judgment to come, on the basis of the principle of uniformity and denial of the biblical account of Creation and the Flood.

Hopefully it has also been shown that it is not 'unscientific' to believe what the Bible says about the origins of the present world.

In this life much can only be theory and many things cannot be explained; finite creatures cannot expect to comprehend fully the handiwork of the infinitely wise and powerful, eternal God. The full story will surely be known in that day when 'every knee shall bow to me (saith the Lord) and every tongue shall confess to God' (Rom.14.11; see also Isa.45.23; Phil.2.11; Rev.1.7). In the meantime in looking at the wonders of nature, the true findings of science enable the believer to say even more today than ever before: 'I am fearfully and wonderfully made' (Psa.139.14) 'O Lord, how manifold are thy works! in wisdom hast thou made them all: the earth is full of thy riches.' (Psa.104.24).

THE CHEMISTRY OF LIFE

A simplified summary of some key aspects is given below:

Cells.

Living organisms are made up of microscopic cells; the human embryo starts as a single cell but a grown body consists of hundreds of millions, or more, cells. Each cell could be likened to a highly sophisticated, automated factory which performs a particular function in the body; for example it may be tissue, a brain cell or part of an eye lens. The cell is enclosed within a membrane through which it can take in the materials it needs and dispose of those it does not need. It contains many components performing a large range of tasks necessary to perform its main function and to maintain itself and to reproduce.

Proteins.

Amongst the most important building blocks of the cells are the 'proteins'. There are many different proteins; it is estimated that there are at least 2000 different proteins in each cell; the cell is programmed to manufacture each protein at the exact moment when it is required. The proteins perform a wide range of functions from those of passive structural material to complex active roles; a few well-known examples of the latter type include insulin, haemoglobin and the enzymes. Each living organism requires its own set of proteins, many of them unique to its 'kind'; there are, therefore, a vast number of proteins. Each one consists of a giant molecule made up of a large number of 'amino acids' (usually several hundred) in a precise combination and unique structure.

Amino acids.

These are complex molecules which are derived, by the digestive process, from the proteins in food. Enzymes are a key factor in this process; they are so efficient that they can accomplish at body temperatures in a few hours what could only be done in the laboratory in a much longer time with concentrated acid at high temperatures. The supply of amino acids depends ultimately, via the food chain, on the capability of plants to synthesise complex food molecules from simple inorganic materials, primarily air and water, using sunlight as the agency.

DNA.

Each cell is controlled by information which it inherits. While the cell system as a whole is now believed to be responsible for heredity and development the main central store of information in the cell is in its nucleus, in another giant molecule. The active part of this consists of 'DNA' (deoxyribonucleic acid). The DNA performs an analogous function to the programme in a computer memory. Almost every individual cell contains all the information necessary to define the complete creature; there is more information stored in the DNA of a single cell than in a large encyclopaedia.

RNA.

An 'RNA' (ribonucleic acid) messenger system communicates the information as required to the various operations within the cell. The RNA also plays a vital part in the reproduction of the DNA and an error detection and correction system ensures that this is done with a degree of accuracy far exceeding that which modern computers achieve. This accuracy, together with the fact that individuals with harmful mutations are not usually fertile, ensures that the precise characteristics of each 'kind' are maintained through many generations.

Genetic code.

The DNA of a cell may be thought of as a complete encyclopaedia. Using this analogy words of 3 letters each identify an amino acid in accordance with a key known as the 'genetic code'. In this alphabet there are only 4 different letters which are known as 'bases' or 'nucleotides'. A paragraph of words specifies the exact sequence of amino acids required to assemble a protein. Thousands of words are grouped together into a chapter known as a 'gene', which is the smallest unit of heredity. Many chapters are combined into a volume called a 'chromosome' and the entire complement of the cell's DNA, known as the 'genome' is made up of a number of such volumes. Almost every human cell contains in its nucleus 23 pairs of chromosomes containing perhaps 3 billion nucleotides on a total of 2 metres of DNA; this is wound on to protein fibres in a complex double spiral which is too small to be seen by the naked eye!

The DNA not only defines the type of organism but also the characteristics of the particular individual. Because of this feature, analysis of the DNA of body cells can show which person they came from; this is known as 'genetic fingerprinting'. Only a very small part of the information contained in the human DNA has so far been explored, but an international £2 billion effort, known as 'The Human Genome Project' was launched in 1988 with the object of 'reading' the entire human life code. Scientists particularly hope to use this information to deal with hereditary diseases. Whilst intentions are good, and some benefits of this kind may well follow, if man acquires the power to alter hereditary characteristics by 'genetic engineering' there will also be tremendous potential for evil. Man's fallen nature is such that almost all new scientific discoveries are put to evil uses as well as to good. Already disputes have arisen over the patent rights to the information resulting from this project.

Overall design.

The whole of this complex chemistry is constructed on only 4 types of DNA base and 20 basic amino acids. It is thought that the amino acids and the genetic code may be universal to all living organisms with rare exceptions. This is claimed to imply that all living organisms have descended from a single pool of primitive cells very early in the process of evolution. There is, however, no satisfactory explanation of how this pool could have originated suddenly, fully developed. To the believer the chemistry of life is further evidence of the truth of the biblical doctrine of one infinitely wise designer, the Creator of all things; the Bible says: 'But now hath God set the members every one of them in the body, as it hath pleased Him' (1 Cor.12.18).

THE AGE OF THE EARTH

Because the 'Big Bang' and evolutionary theories are based on the principle of uniformity they require the whole of creation to be of great age. Estimates for the time since the 'Big Bang' still vary widely within the range from 10 to 20 billion (thousand million) years, while the age of the earth itself in the same scheme is put at about 4500 million years.

The Bible, on the other hand, makes it clear that the earth is of very much more recent origin. Whether Bishop Ussher's date for creation of 4004 B.C. is precisely correct or not, for those who believe the Bible to be without error the age of the earth must be measured in thousands, not millions or billions of years.

There appears to be a widespread impression that scientific evidence all points to a great age for the earth but, in fact, the main arguments for this great age would only appear to be conclusive if the theories of uniformity and evolution were true. There is, moreover, increasing scientific evidence which is consistent with the earth being relatively young.

The main arguments used to support the great age view are:

– evolution itself;

– the time it has taken for light from remote galaxies to reach the earth;

– radioactive dating methods.

These and some of the evidences of a young earth are reviewed below:

1. *Evolution.*

If evolution were indeed a proven fact then presumably the earth would, of necessity, be very old, but as seen in previous chapters evolution is very far from being proven.

2. *Light from remote galaxies.*

Some of the remote galaxies are thought to be at such a distance that light from them takes billions of years to reach the earth; therefore, it is said, they must have existed these billions of years ago. Although this sounds very plausible it ignores the Creator; in any case some of the premises on which this argument is based may be incorrect.

God created the world in a fully developed, working state; Adam was made a grown man with the appearance of age and the trees in Eden had an appearance of age, their fruit was ready to eat. So God could have created the heavenly bodies with their light already flowing; how this was done is not open to scientific investigation any more than how He, as Jesus, exercising the same power, turned the water into good, and therefore apparently old, wine (John 2.1-10 & Luke 5.39).

Secondly, the distances may not be so great. With the exception of the closest stars distances cannot be measured directly and a number of deductions and hypotheses have to be made.

Thirdly the argument assumes that the speed of light has always been what it is today. This seems to be a very reasonable assumption, but it is now being increasingly challenged on scientific grounds.

3. *Radioactivity.*

Uranium, found in certain rocks, decays radioactively by a series of steps, through various forms known as 'isotopes', to become lead. This process occurs at a known rate today. The proportions of the different isotopes present in a rock sample can therefore be used to estimate its age, assuming that the original content is known and assuming that the rate of decay has not changed. This method, whilst far from producing consistent, accurate results, gives very great ages for many rock samples; however, both of the underlying assumptions could be wrong:

– The original content of the rocks at creation could well have been a mixture of isotopes such that after a few thousand years of decay the content would be what is found today. This would be consistent with another indication; this process of radioactive decay gives off helium and the amount of helium in the earth's atmosphere is only sufficient to account for a few thousand years decay at today's rate.

– The rate of decay is assumed to have been constant; this also seems to be a reasonable assumption but there is no long-term evidence to prove that this has been the case. The rate of decay is, in fact, closely related to the speed of light.

Radiocarbon as a means of dating fossils has already been considered in chapter 4 where it was seen that the low radioactivity of the fossils need not imply a very great age; it is fully consistent with them having been formed in the Flood, assuming the water vapour canopy was present originally.

Microscopic pieces of radioactive uranium and polonium were embedded in coal deposits found in Colorado. The effects which they left in the surrounding material can best be explained on the basis that the coal was formed very quickly and comparatively recently. This would be the case if they were formed in the Flood, whereas it is very difficult to reconcile this effect with slow formation millions of years ago.

Likewise small pieces of very short life radioactive polonium in granite rocks have left effects which are compatible with the rocks having been created with the polonium in place; they are very difficult to explain if the rocks cooled from liquid over millions of years in accordance with uniformitarian theory.

4. *The temperature of the moons.*

The moons of the planets are relatively small and on the assumption that they were formed 4500 million years ago it was for long supposed that they would have cooled down and become inactive. In recent years, however, signs of activity have been detected on the earth's moon which appear to be associated with a hot interior. More spectacularly, in 1979 the Voyager space probe witnessed volcanic eruptions on Io, one of the moons of Jupiter. Various possible reasons have been proposed for these unexpected observations, but relatively recent creation would be a good explanation.

5. *Cosmic particles.*

Meteoric dust and meteorites fall on the earth and moon. On the moon there is no wind or weather to disturb the dust and it accumulates. Before the first moon landing it was generally supposed that in 4500 million years a layer of loose dust anything up to 50 metres deep would have built up. In the event the men who landed on the moon in 1969 found a few millimetres of dust, consistent with the age of the moon being a few thousand years.

On earth the number of meteorites found in the rocks is far less than would be expected if they had been falling on the earth at the current rate for millions of years.

6. *Salt in the sea.*

Salt is continually being washed into the sea; if this process had been going on at the present rate for millions of years the sea should contain far more salt, even if it started with none; if it started saline then there is an even larger discrepancy. It is the view of many marine biologists that the sea always contained salt and doubtless God would have made the sea at Creation sufficiently saline to match the needs of the creatures He put in it. If the oceans are 'young', there is no discrepancy.

7. *The ancient trees.*

The oldest known living things on earth are trees in North America. The bristle cone pine is a peculiar stunted tree which gives the appearance of being a living fossil. 17 of the oldest known examples of this species have been shown to be over 4000 years old from a count of their rings. These trees are immune to disease and pest attack and appear to live indefinitely; there are no signs of remains of earlier specimens. These trees therefore may be the first generation which grew up after the Flood had destroyed their predecessors. Likewise some of the giant sequoias, which are well over 3000 years old, and grow in quite a different environment, tend to point to a similar conclusion.

8. *Archaeology and history.*

Archaeology, history and the Bible all point to civilisation beginning in the Near or Middle East and on roughly the same time-scales. Somewhat earlier dates are ascribed to some primitive remains, usually based on radiocarbon methods, but in any case neither archaeology nor history know of anything beyond a few thousand years ago.

There are other scientific arguments for a young earth, some of them more technical; these may be found in the literature quoted in Appendix C.

FURTHER READING

There are, today, many books on different aspects of this subject varying in technical depth and degree of detail; new books continue to appear frequently. The following list is of necessity a selection; it includes those sources which have been most helpful in preparation of this booklet and concentrates mainly on authors who believe in the literal truth of the record in the Bible.

Every reader should find much that is clear in each of these books but the nature of the subject is such that some of the material will be appreciated best by those with some scientific background. An asterisk marks those titles where such a background is likely to be most helpful.

J.C.Whitcomb. *The Early Earth.* Baker Book House.

*L.R.Croft. *How Life Began.* Evangelical Press.

R.D.G.Price. *In the Beginning.* New Wine Press.

J.W.Milner. *Creation in Six Days.* Gospel Tidings Vol.3.

D.T.Gish. *Evolution: The Challenge of the Fossil Record.* Creation-Life Publishers.

D.Rosevear. *Creation Science.* New Wine Press.

*M.Bowden. *Science vs. Evolution.* Sovereign Publications

*M.Bowden. *Ape Men: Fact or Fallacy.* Sovereign Publications.

*J.C.Whitcomb and H.M.Morris. *The Genesis Flood.* Baker Book House. (This is the classic work on the scientific interpretation of the observed facts on the basis of the literal truth of the Bible record.)

Further Reading

W.W.Greenman. *Evidences of the Flood.* Gospel Standard Trust.

D.C.C.Watson. *The Great Brain Robbery.* Published by the author.

P.D.Ackerman. *It's a Young World After All.* Baker Book House.

J.C.Whitcomb and D.B.DeYoung. *The Moon: Its Creation, Form and Significance.* Baker Book House.

D.B.DeYoung. *Astronomy and the Bible.* Baker Book House.

D.M.MacKay. *Brains, Machines and Persons.* Collins.

*M.Denton. *Evolution: a Theory in Crisis.* Burnett Books.

M.Pitman. *Adam and Evolution.* Rider.

(The latter two books, by authors who do not acknowledge Biblical Creation, refute evolutionary theories on purely scientific grounds. These books and *Brains, Machines and Persons* are available in some public libraries.)

Regular Publications;

Origins. Biblical Creation Society, P.O.Box 22, Rugby, CV22 7SY.

Creation. Creation Science Movement, 50 Brecon Ave., Portsmouth, PO6 2AW.

God's Wonderful World. Monthly article in: Cheering Words, 22 Victoria Road, Stamford, PE9 1HB.